EXPLOSIVES &
ARSON INVESTIGATION

SOLVING CRIMES WITH SCIENCE:
Forensics

EXPLOSIVES & ARSON INVESTIGATION

Jean Ford

Mason Crest

Mason Crest
450 Parkway Drive, Suite D
Broomall, PA 19008
www.masoncrest.com

Printed and bound in the United States of America.

First printing
9 8 7 6 5 4 3 2 1

Series ISBN: 978-1-4222-2861-6
ISBN: 978-1-4222-2867-8
ebook ISBN: 978-1-4222-8953-2

The Library of Congress has cataloged the
hardcopy format(s) as follows:

Library of Congress Cataloging-in-Publication Data

Ford, Jean (Jean Otto)
   Explosives & arson investigation / Jean Ford.
      p. cm. — (Solving crimes with science, forensics)
   Audience: 012.
   Audience: Grades 7 to 8.
   Includes index.
   ISBN 978-1-4222-2867-8 (hardcover) — ISBN 978-1-4222-2861-6 (series) — ISBN 978-1-4222-8953-2
(ebook)
   1. Arson investigation—Juvenile literature. 2. Fires—Juvenile literature. 3. Explosions—Juvenile literature. 4. Forensic sciences—Juvenile literature. I. Title. II. Title: Explosives and arson investigation.
   HV8079.A7F67 2014
   363.25'9642—dc23
                                        2013006939

Produced by Vestal Creative Services.
www.vestalcreative.com

Contents

Introduction

By Jay A. Siegel, Ph.D.
Director, Forensic and Investigative Sciences Program
Indiana University, Purdue University, Indianapolis

It seems like every day the news brings forth another story about crime in the United States. Although the crime rate has been slowly decreasing over the past few years (due perhaps in part to the aging of the population), crime continues to be a very serious problem. Increasingly, the stories we read that involve crimes also mention the role that forensic science plays in solving serious crimes. Sensational crimes provide real examples of the power of forensic science. In recent years there has been an explosion of books, movies, and TV shows devoted to forensic science and crime investigation. The wondrously successful *CSI* TV shows have spawned a major increase in awareness of and interest in forensic science as a tool for solving crimes. *CSI* even has its own syndrome: the "*CSI* Effect," wherein jurors in real cases expect to hear testimony about science such as fingerprints, DNA, and blood spatter because they saw it on TV.

The unprecedented rise in the public's interest in forensic science has fueled demands by students and parents for more educational programs that teach the applications of science to crime. This started in colleges and universities but has filtered down to high schools and middle schools. Even elementary school students now learn how science is used in the criminal justice system. Most educators agree that this developing interest in forensic science is a good thing. It has provided an excellent opportunity to teach students science—and they have fun learning it! Forensic science is an ideal vehicle for teaching science for several reasons. It is truly multidisciplinary; practically every field of science has forensic applications. Successful forensic scientists must be good problem solvers and critical thinkers. These are critical skills that all students need to develop.

In all of this rush to implement forensic science courses in secondary schools throughout North America, the development of grade-appropriate resources that help guide students and teachers is seriously lacking. This new series: *Solving Crimes With Science: Forensics* is important and timely. Each book in the series contains a concise, age-appropriate discussion of one or more areas of forensic science.

Students are never too young to begin to learn the principles and applications of science. Forensic science provides an interesting and informative way to introduce scientific concepts in a way that grabs and holds the students' attention. *Solving Crimes With Science: Forensics* promises to be an important resource in teaching forensic science to students twelve to eighteen years old.

Igniting Interest: The Basics

South Orange, New Jersey. January 19, 2000. Pumper trucks responded in mere minutes. Once firefighters "laid the lines," it took even less time to put out the flames. Firefighters were able to contain the blaze to just one room—a third-floor lounge of six-story Boland Hall—yet bodies of students dotted the hallways of the freshmen dorm.

In the wee hours of that chilly, winter morning, Seton Hall University, a Catholic college fifteen miles (24 kilometers) southwest of New York City, earned the unwanted distinction of having one of the worst dormitory fires in recent U.S. history. Three students died in the 1,500-plus-degree blaze. Six area hospitals treated at least fifty-eight others for burns, smoke inhalation, broken bones (from jumping out windows), and other injuries. And the fire wasn't any accident; two students started it as a prank.

Queens County, New York. Ash Wednesday, 1995. A firefighter guided police detectives through the steaming, dripping, black debris of a house fire. The three made their way down a narrow staircase to a dank basement where, in the eerie glow of flashlight beams, a half-scorched woman lay on the soaked, unfinished floor. She lay on her side, eerily frozen in the sitting position in which she'd been tied. Her hands remained behind her back, but flames had removed the bindings and the chair to which she'd been bound. Firefighters had stumbled upon the twenty-year-old victim of a kidnapping-for-ransom gone horribly wrong.

Prairie Village, Kansas. October 24, 1995. Autumn winds relentlessly pummeled 7517 Canterbury Court, quickly fueling an inferno. Alarms sounded in Station Number 2 at 12:25 a.m. The ladder company arrived at the fire scene just six minutes later. Additional companies responded nearly as quickly, and the residential fire was "tapped" (put out) by approximately 1:45 a.m. Despite the quick response and heroic measures by firefighters, two children lay dead among the home's ashes. Their mother had made sure they would.

What do these three cases have in common? Fire was the weapon of choice; the cases each took months—even years—to close; and forensic science solved them all. That's where the similarities end.

In the Seton Hall example, students set the fire to get even with a dorm staff member. Kidnappers lit the second fire to cover up the accidental death of their hostage. The third fire was also intentional—a bitter wife's attempt at murder-by-arson; she burned her kids to get even with their dad. Forensics was able to bring the cases to their conclusion.

Fingerprints, a stray hair, fibers, DNA, cigarette butts, even a single gum wrapper are typical of clues that provide forensic evidence in criminal

Fast Fact:
Fire and Explosions

All forms of fire and explosion are subtypes of "combustion."

cases. Fire and bombs usually destroy them, however. What role can forensics play when explosions or flames ravage evidence? That's where fire investigators and science come in.

Seton Hall

In the Seton Hall University dorm fire, for example, fire investigators worked backward from the area of least destruction to greatest. When investigators locate the most severe fire damage, they've usually found the "place of origin" (where the fire started). In this case, a couch in the third-floor lounge and its immediate surroundings suffered the heaviest damage. Conclusion: the fire started there.

Fire investigators then checked for signs of any fire-starting fuels like gasoline, lighter fluid, or other flammable substances used to help fires burn. Burn patterns on the floor of the lounge proved that such **accelerants** weren't used, but at least two witnesses reported seeing a "campfire-sized blaze" of construction paper on one of the three couches in the lounge. Forensic tests on samples of the area's ashes confirmed their reports.

Investigators also diagrammed the fire scene, marking where the fire started, the progression of smoke and fire damage, and where the injured and dead lay in relationship to the fire's point of origin. Forensic medical exams and autopsies detailed each victim's condition. These facts, cold as they seem, helped determine smoke and heat intensity at specific times and places, what burned, and the paths fire and smoke each took and how quickly.

Within nine months of the deadly blaze, investigators had a good idea of what happened. To confirm their theory, they enlisted the help of the National Institute of Standards and Technology and built almost-perfect models of the Boland Hall lounge, down to flooring and couch materials.

Investigators simulated the Seton Hall dorm fire to study how the fire burned.

Then they burned the life-sized replicas, three times no less, comparing what they saw in each experiment with timelines constructed from survivors' testimonies and crime-scene evidence. They recorded all three burns on videotape, showing how the fire burned.

Every fire needs three elements in order to burn: an energy source to ignite it (heat, spark, friction, electrical current, intense light, open flame, etc.), fuel (something that burns), and oxygen. Take away any one element and the result is no fire. What forensic science couldn't prove was if the construction paper caught fire accidentally, or if someone deliberately set it on fire. Investigators were missing the ignition source and motive, if any existed.

Witness interviews and police wiretaps of suspects' phone lines filled in those gaps. One suspect—Joseph LePore—reportedly admitted setting the fire as he talked with his sister months later. Investigators got the confession on tape. The Boland Hall fire was a case of arson.

Arson is the willful and *malicious* burning of any property for an improper or illegal purpose. By definition, it's intentional. Apparently the tragedy at Boland Hall began with two residents, a resident assistant (RA) against whom they held a grudge, and a construction-paper banner the RA had posted welcoming freshmen back from Christmas break.

Student interviews revealed tension did indeed exist between Dan Nugent, the RA, and suspect Joseph LePore and another dorm resident, Sean Ryan. Just a few weeks before the fire, Nugent had written up LePore and Ryan for suspicion of marijuana use in their rooms. On the night of the fire, Nugent warned them twice about excessive rowdiness. Two friends—Tino Cataldo and Michael Karpenski—witnessed Ryan tear down Nugent's six-foot (1.8-meter) banner to spite the RA, but security videos prove Cataldo and Karpenski left the dorm about an hour before LePore set it on fire. Although those two weren't involved in lighting the fire, all four conspired the next day to never mention the banner to investigators.

Ryan allegedly admitted he saw the fire on the couch the night of the fire, but wouldn't tell who set it. He knocked on just one door, Dan Nugent's, to alert him. Then Ryan grabbed LePore, and the two fled down a back staircase. They warned no one else. Neither teen realized how combustible the couch was or how hot and toxically it would burn. The result: three innocent freshmen died from toxic fumes and dense smoke, and scores were injured.

It took over forty months' worth of investigation, forensic tests, witness interviews, and other techniques to gather enough evidence to file charges. In June 2003, prosecutors charged Ryan and LePore with sixty counts, including arson, reckless manslaughter, felony murder, and conspiring a cover-up. The indictment also charged a third student—Santino "Tino" Cataldo—and others with obstruction of justice for failing to tell investigators what they knew.

Forensics helped solve this case despite the loss of traditional evidence like fingerprints and hair fibers. Point-of-origin, burn patterns, the lack of accelerant, trace evidence in the ashes, and forensic autopsies all pointed to a deliberately set fire started in a pile of construction paper on a particular couch in a specific room. These facts set the stage for the interviews that ultimately solved the questions of suspects and motive.

Problems of Investigating Fires and Explosions

Not all arson cases are as obvious as the Seton Hall fire. Fires, of course, have many causes. That's the first challenge. Natural triggers (like lightning), manmade ones (whether accidental or deliberate), hosts of mechanical, structural, substantive, and electrical triggers can all cause fires—and

Saving lives always takes priority over preserving evidence.

First, Ms. Daniels spent weeks surfing the the Internet to learn how to burn a body beyond recognition and how to fool arson investigators. Next, she meticulously created a new identity for her husband Clayton Daniels: a new name (Jake Gregg), new birth certificate, new Social Security number, new Texas driver's license, and so on. Finally, three days before her husband was to go to jail on unrelated charges, the two dug up a corpse from a cemetery for people who cannot afford burial plots or have little or no

Igniting Interest: The Basics   **17**

family, buckled it into Clayton's car, let the car roll off the cliff, poured char-coal lighter fluid all over the body and vehicle, and lit the wreck on fire.

"Clayton Daniels" was no more. Everyone thought he died in the accident. His jail order was stamped "deceased." Coworkers attended his funeral and raised money for his widow and children. A few weeks later, Molly introduced the kids to her new boyfriend, Jake Gregg. Interestingly, the guy looked just like Clayton, but with black hair.

Investigators were suspicious from the start. The road leading to where the car went over the cliff had no skid marks or any other signs of a high-speed crash. The driver's seat was the hottest spot of the fire; it wouldn't be in an accident. Burn patterns indicated accelerant use. Trace evidence of lighter fluid in the wreckage confirmed it. Finally, the DNA from the body didn't match samples taken from Clayton's mother, so the person who died in the crash could not have been her son.

After a superficial examination of the scene, this case could have been easy to write off as an accident. But on closer inspection, it quickly became obvious that the evidence pointed to something far more ghoulish. Sherlock Holmes was absolutely correct when he stated, "It is a capital mistake to theorize before one has data."

Even with sound theory based on solid evidence, arson cases are the least often and least effectively prosecuted criminal cases across America. According to a 2005 article from InterFIRE, an internationally recognized professional fire-investigation organization, the "clearance rate" (the rate at which cases are investigated, prosecuted, and closed) is under 10 percent in the United States, and the conviction rate is even worse: less than 1 percent for arson and bombing prosecutions. Statistically speaking, that means that someone considering setting off a bomb or starting a fire in the United States has a 99 percent chance of getting away with it. Arson is extremely hard to prove.

What Are the Odds . . . ?

of an arson case in Canada never making it to trial: 80 in 100*
of an arson case in the U.S. never making it to trial: 96 in 100**
of getting away with arson in the U.S.: 99 in 100**

(Sources: *British Columbia Lottery Corp., British Columbia's Partnership for Responsible Gambling, and Blaze: The Forensics Fire by Nicholas Faith. **U.S. National Safety Council, U.S. National Center for Health Statistics, and the U.S. Census Bureau.)

Besides evidence loss inherent to fires and explosions and the temptation to theorize before obtaining forensic support, the act of arson is **clandestine** by nature. Arsonists often commit their work under cover of night and almost always far from curious eyes. Witnesses are rare. Additionally, many arsonists execute their crimes with calculated planning and alibis made possible with timers used to ignite bombs and start fires. (For instance, a bomb goes off just as the culprit is sitting down to a very public dinner or a fire starts while the arsonist is in a meeting.) For all these reasons, evidence pointing to specific suspects is almost always circumstantial, and any criminal attorney will tell you that circumstantial cases are the hardest to prosecute.

Fire and Bomb Investigations

Many fires are accidental, like when someone falls asleep while smoking or a portable heater is too close to beds or curtains. To prevent such tragedies from recurring, it becomes as important to understand accidental fires as it is to understand criminal ones. If, for instance, investigators find that a specific coffeemaker accidentally started a fire because of thermostat defects, then manufacturers can recall that item before anyone else has the same problem. If a fire started because someone put gasoline in a kerosene heater or a family tried heating their home with a gas stove, then officials

Accidental car fires usually do not originate in the driver's seat.

know they need to educate the pubic to prevent similar mistakes. Forensics can determine "cause" in such cases.

If authorities discover somebody deliberately set a fire or explosion, they can look at possible motives, suspects, and similar incidents. If they conclude the case was isolated (as they did in the opening examples), the priority becomes identifying who set the fire and why. If detectives think a fire or bombing is just one of a series of similar acts—the work of a serial arsonist or bomber—it becomes essential to understand cause and method in order to spot patterns, develop profiles, and intercept the culprit before he or she can do more harm. Whatever the scenario, investigators must rule out accidental causes first.

Many arsonists deliberately set buildings ablaze for insurance money or to cover up crimes. A few light fires or set off explosions just for the thrill of it. Even political causes can drive criminals. Whatever the cause, arson and explosion investigators and the forensic techniques they use are essential to interpreting what little evidence is left at the crime scene.

Obviously, intentional fire-setting and bombings are criminal acts. By definition, they involve the law. Some accidental circumstances also cross into the legal realm, especially those involving insurance claims or civil cases. That's where forensic science comes in.

Forensic Science

Forensic science is any science applied to questions whose answers have legal ramifications. Our word "forensic" originates from the Latin word forensis, which literally translates "of the forum"; legal proceedings of ancient Rome took place in the forum. Forensic (an adjective) came to mean "connected with or pertaining to courts of law." Forensics (with an s) is the noun.

Many sciences have forensic aspects. For example, most of us are familiar with odontology or dentistry; forensic odontology is the application of dentistry to legal matters, such as identifying a corpse through dental records or comparing bite wounds to a suspect's teeth. Geology is the study of the earth, its rocks and soils; forensic geology applies to legal matters such as "typing" the soil on a suspect's shoe or under a victim's fingernails and then isolating its origin, thereby determining that that shoe or body has been in a specific location.

Other forensic fields include forensic psychology (minds, including criminal profiling), forensic serology (blood/body fluids), forensic entomology (insects), forensic anthropology (skeletons/bones), forensic toxicology (drugs/poisons), forensic ballistics (firearms/bullets/gunpowder), forensic graphology (handwriting), forensic dactyloscopy (fingerprints), and even forensic art (facial reproductions based on actual skulls and anthropology). Clearly, career possibilities in forensic science vary as much as the crimes they try to solve.

The Principal Players

Those who actually investigate fires vary with circumstances. In bombings, local officials automatically notify (and defer to) national agencies. In the United States, the U.S. Department of Justice's Bureau of Alcohol, Tobacco, Firearms, and Explosives (ATF) takes over. Canada's equivalents include the Criminal Investigative Analysis Unit of the Royal Canadian Mounted Police (RCMP), among others. Local officials assist.

If fatalities occur, the coroner's office and morgue get involved. If a fire hides another crime, then fire officials call in police detectives. When fire deaths involve interstate kidnapping (or other federal offenses), as it did in the second example cited at the beginning of this chapter, the Federal

Forensic anthropology involves the study of bones to uncover facts of a crime.

Bureau of Investigation (FBI) steps in. For simple fires (without fatalities), local fire investigators are in charge, but the district attorney's investigators, local law enforcement, insurance company personnel, private investigators, forensic technicians, and even engineering experts (chemical, mechanical, electrical, and fire) may get involved, especially if arson is suspected.

Many of these agencies have their own arson units. Considering the potential variety of people who can be involved in fire and explosion investigations, uniform guidelines for documenting scenes and collecting

Police officers, firefighters, paramedics, and forensic scientists may all be at the scene of a fire.

EXPLOSIVES & ARSON INVESTIGATION

evidence have become critical to the investigative process. The U.S. Department of Justice's National Institute of Justice with the University of Central Florida's National Center for Forensic Science has produced such guidelines in their handbook Fire and Arson Scene Evidence: A Guide for Public Safety Personnel. Many of the techniques detailed in the following chapters are based on these methods. The first guidelines address what forensic investigators encounter when they initially arrive at a fire or bomb scene.

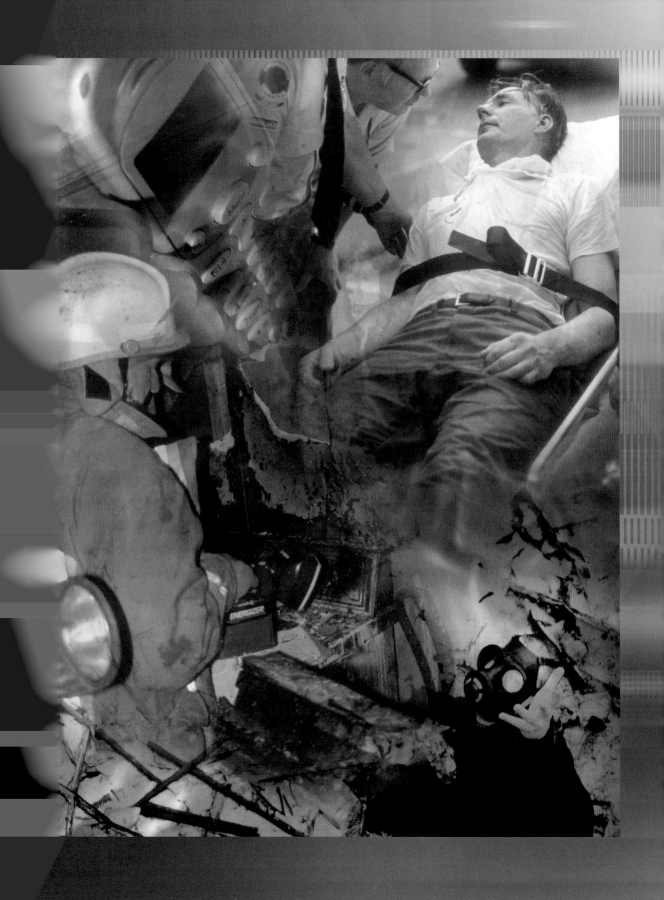

Where There's Smoke...: The Scene

Johnson County, Indiana. December 2003. Mike Vergon arrives at the scene of a recent fire. An investigator with the ATF, Vergon is lending a hand to local fire investigators working on a series of arson fires that have consumed a variety of structures in the Indianapolis area—five fires, to be exact, in just two weeks. The blaze is out now, but Vergon's job is just beginning. After examining the charred structure, the evidence is clear: he's looking at arson number six.

Bergen County, New Jersey. March 2004. It's 5:30 in the morning, and the ringing of a cell phone breaks through the haze of morning slumber. A fire has just ravaged a local apartment building, destroying a ground-floor business and leaving forty residents homeless. Arson detective Gary Allmers rushes to the scene. Wearing a helmet and protective jumpsuit, he enters the burned-out shell. Hours later, he emerges with a verdict: this fire was accidental.

Two fires. Two investigators. Two very different conclusions. Yet both men drew their conclusions from mere ashes. Most people would wonder how.

"The scene tells you a lot," asserts Detective Gary Allmers in the 2004 Record (Bergen County, N.J.) article "Arson or Accident: Fire Investigators Find Answers in Ashes" by Raghuram Vadarevu. Evidence is everywhere to trained eyes.

"Interviews help and can point us in a certain direction," adds Bergen arson detective Thomas Dionsio, "but it's the physical evidence at the fire scene that tells us."

Examining the Scene: Bergen County Apartment Fire

Allmers has already learned from eyewitness accounts that the apartment fire raged most fiercely in the back of a ground-floor laundry business, a good indicator of its point of origin. The detective starts there. Only the first-floor ceiling in the back has collapsed, and the deepest charring scars that area. Finding less damage to walls and appliances in the front of the shop, Allmers confirms that the fire burned longest and hottest on the rear ground floor. His witnesses were right.

Next, Allmers works through upper levels of the building, one floor at a time. He pays close attention to indications of heat intensity and fire and smoke damage along the way. Allmers knows that fires typically spread up and sideways from where they start, and that specific parts of a building can impact that tendency. A stairwell, for instance, draws fire its way be-

CAREER SPOTLIGHT:
Fire Investigator vs. Arson Detective

Fire investigators do exactly what their name suggests: investigate fires regardless of cause—natural, accidental, or intentional. They determine the causes and call in arson detectives if they suspect someone intentionally set the blaze. Fire investigators usually work for the fire department and are often former firefighters.

Arson detectives also do what their name suggests: examine fires, but only in cases of arson. They have received training in detecting unnatural, intentional, and manmade causes of fires. These forensic detectives look for and gather criminal evidence to support law enforcement and legal proceedings.

cause of the extra oxygen its drafts provide. Open windows do the same. Even air pockets between walls can suck flames in their direction. Understanding how fire moves is critical to correctly interpreting any fire scene.

On the third floor, Allmers observes that flames crept inside apartment walls, heading for air; scorch marks on framing inside the walls give it away. Because fire seeks oxygen and always burns up, he theorizes that the fire took that path—through the walls—to the roof, where, fed by fresh air, it grew more fierce and consumed the tar roof, collapsing it onto the fourth floor.

Allmers is now pretty sure he knows where the fire started and the path it took. But how did it start? Returning to the first floor, he looks again at

als including glass, porcelain, iron, and aluminum; the reaction of window glass to heat; even the undersides of charred furniture. According to the U.S. Fire Administration's fire investigation manual, these are all details to which arson investigators need to pay careful attention.

Vergon does. After hours of painstaking observation, and without releasing any specific evidence to support his conclusion (for fear of compromising an ongoing investigation), Vergon confirms his suspicions. This is another case of arson. Suddenly, the investigation turns from determining cause to determining who started it. "The way these fires are set, we have a general idea of who we're looking for."

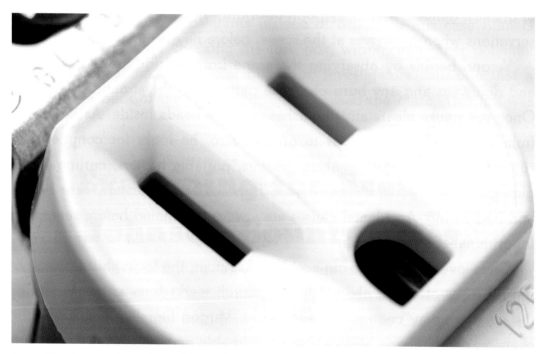

Investigators rule out accidental causes of a fire—like a faulty electrical socket—before searching for criminal evidence.

Anatomy of Fire-Scene Investigation: First Responders

A thorough fire-/bomb-scene analysis doesn't actually begin with investigators like Vergon and Allmers. It starts with the "first responders" as they approach and arrive at the scene. They are usually the first to arrive at a fire or explosion—hence the name "first responders"—and can include firefighters, police officers, bomb squads, and paramedics. They often provide the most critical clues.

First responders are trained to pay attention to vehicles and persons leaving the scene of a fire; any unusual activity in the area; flame and smoke conditions (color, height, direction, and volume); unusual odors; and the presence, location, and condition of victims, witnesses, and bystanders. They also learn to note relevant weather factors; structural conditions (lights on/off, windows open/closed, doors locked/unlocked, fire escapes, garages, etc.); the locations of utilities; the positions of switches, valves, and timers; any peculiarities (like stacked furniture); odd debris or suspicious containers; and the status of smoke alarms and sprinkler systems. In the case of car fires, they look at similar details (as they apply to vehicles), plus road conditions, traffic volume, and so on.

At an active site—one where a fire is still burning—safety becomes the overriding concern. First responders identify dangers like unstable debris, combustible materials, weakened structures, areas at risk, or even suspected incendiary or explosive devices. They share that information with later-arriving personnel. First responders use road blocks and the famous yellow tape to establish safety zones for victims, witnesses, public safety workers, investigators, and onlookers. They also set up a security perimeter to control all access to the scene. First responders establish control of the scene.

Emergency operations at fire and bomb scenes can eventually involve many different agencies and organizations. Therefore, first responders must quickly establish a command post, a primary contact person, lines of communication, and the chain of authority. These actions are not only critical to saving lives and successfully suppressing fires and explosives; they also set the stage for the post-fire investigation.

If victims (or possible victims) remain inside a fire or bomb site, rescuing them becomes the number-one priority while containing the danger. Both efforts destroy evidence, but saving lives always outweighs preserving evidence. Emergency crews know that. They're well aware of how rescue, fire **suppression**, overhaul (the process of opening concealed spaces to

While the fire burns, first responders safeguard the area to prevent further injury or death.

Historical First Responders

- In 1801, the first fire hydrants appeared on Philadelphia streets, but they weren't for just anyone to use. Local fire companies hired big brutes to guard the hydrants so rival companies couldn't use them. These plug-guards (or "plug-uglies") were tough thugs who didn't mind breaking a few bones to keep the competition from using their water. They were often the first on the scene.
- Early fire trucks were horse-drawn rigs. In those days horse thieves were also common, but if you had a dalmatian, you had a living, breathing burglar alarm. Dalmatians love horses and will fiercely protect them, so when fire companies started using horses to pull their rigs, these dogs were a must. Dalmatians have been the unofficial mascot to fire companies ever since.
- A woman named Molly Williams is the first American female firefighter on record. She lived in the late 1700s.

(Source: *Fire!* by Joy Masoff)

find pockets of fire and remove smoldering material), and salvage efforts (the process of protecting, moving, or removing items) damage potential evidence. Most personnel take whatever steps they can to preserve evidence without compromising the safety of victims or rescuers.

For example, a police officer might notice tool marks around a lock (a sign of forced entry) as fire engulfs the door. Or a sliding glass entrance

Standard Stuff

Most first responders carry standard equipment and tools for securing a scene and preserving preliminary evidence. The minimum kit should include:

- barrier tape
- large road cones, flares, or flashers
- lights (flashlights and spotlights)
- personal protective equipment (special clothing, helmet, boots, safety shield)
- gloves (disposable and/or work gloves)
- hand tools (crowbar, hammer, screwdriver, wrench, brushes, trowel)
- large tools (axe, spade, rake, broom, saw, drill with wood or metal bits)
- electrical tools (wire cutters, strippers, and gauge; volt/amp/ohm meter, tester)
- cutting tools (bolt cutters, carpet cutters, pipe cutter, utility knife, pocket knife)
- decontamination equipment (buckets, pans, neutralizing agents)
- writing equipment (notebooks, pens, pencils, permanent markers)
- clean, unused evidence containers (bags, jars, cans)

- evidence tags, labels, and tape
- evidence place-markers (cones, flags, tent cards)
- tape measure
- compass
- photographic equipment
- means of communication (cell phone, walkie-talkies, radio)

While this list does cover the very basic tools first responders need, fire investigators need all these plus more. The U.S. Fire Administration's Basic Tools and Resources for Fire Investigators: A Handbook lists over 150 items in its "Fire Investigation Tools and Equipment List."

(Sources: The National Institute of Justice and the National Center for Forensic Science's handbook Fire and Arson Scene Evidence and the U.S. Fire Administration's Basic Tools and Resources for Fire Investigators: A Handbook)

won't budge because someone jammed a stick in its track; then rescuers shatter the door to save the victim and flames consume the stick. Or a body lies at the base of a stairway before firefighters carry it outside. Many first responders make mental notes of such details as they work the scene and later document them in written reports. These notes can make or break a case.

Some evidence is naturally "*transient* evidence" like footprints in mud, drag marks in snow, or evaporating liquids on a garage floor. Some can be as fleeting as odors or odd-colored smoke. First responders know some evidence won't survive the fire—but snapping a quick photo, jotting brief notes, or even making audiotaped observations at the scene can preserve evidence long after it has disappeared.

Anatomy of Fire-Scene Investigation: Post-Fire Investigative Personnel

The blaze is out, and an uncanny calm settles on the scene. Only a soggy, sooty mess remains. Most of us wouldn't have a clue where to begin. To fire investigators, it's simple. Their job is not to put out the blaze or rescue people. The focus is recovery of evidence and, if applicable, bodies.

Who exactly makes up this group of investigators varies with the size and cause of a fire, the extent of damage, and if there are any victims, but a team of players always works a post-blaze scene, and that team usually employs far more than the three or four investigators routinely seen on TV shows. Multiple fire and police units (each with unique areas of expertise); the coroner or morgue's office; legal investigators working for county, state, or provincial agencies; and even national investigators can be on site. In larger fires, explosions, arson cases, and incidents involving casualties, officials may form a task force of national, state, and local fire and law enforcement personnel who work together to solve the case.

When they first arrive, all investigators check in with those in charge of the scene. They meet quickly to identify other personnel on site, adjust the chain of authority if necessary, establish legal "right of entry" (access to the scene), evaluate the area's safety, and determine what additional personnel or resources are required to process the scene. (Note: investigators can't just rush in. Like police detectives, fire and bomb investigators must follow laws concerning entering a property and conducting a search—not to mention seizing evidence—particularly if they know arson or another crime is involved.) Working with first responders, investigators might also reassess and redefine the perimeter. Those are the first steps.

Next, most investigators will interview witnesses, victims (if still there), first responders, and first-in firefighters before entering the ruins themselves. Fire investigators might also talk with later-arriving personnel, the person who reported the incident, the last to get out, any bystanders or neighbors, and property owners. Sometimes the smallest detail, the most seemingly insignificant information from witnesses at the time, provides a critical clue.

Once a fire is put out, investigators can search the scene for clues.

Where There's Smoke...: The Scene

The importance of witnesses was crucial to solving the Prairie Village, Kansas, house fire that killed two children (described at the beginning of chapter 1). One of the clues that led to Debora Green's ultimate arrest and conviction came from details investigators observed when interviewing witnesses before they set foot in the house. One of the witnesses was Green herself, who was interviewed as a victim and property owner. Her hair was wet at the scene—as if she'd just stepped out of a shower—and appeared to have been recently cut. The neighbors to whom she ran "for help" affirmed that's how she looked when she frantically arrived at their doorstep.

If this woman truly woke up to smoke after being asleep for at least an hour and then immediately fled the house without encountering any flames (as she claimed), when would she have had time to shower and cut her hair—and why would she? Prosecutors later proved from her hair samples that Green had been close enough to flames to singe the ends of her hair. That's a common mistake arsonists make.

Many amateur arsonists underestimate the power of accelerants and suffer burns or minor injuries when the fire "flashes" on ignition. Green scorched her hair when she lit the lighter fluid she had spread along an upstairs hallway just outside the children's rooms, down the steps (this area was most heavily soaked—the kids could never have escaped that way), and finally across the first floor to just outside her bedroom. When she lit the accelerant's trail, she thought of it as a fuse and assumed she had time to quickly and safely shut her door. Instead, the fire flashed when she lit it, and flames shot toward her face and singed her hair. She ran to her bathroom, forgetting to shut her door (a critical error), doused her head with water and quickly cut off any singed hair before fleeing the house through the exterior door off her bedroom. Debora Green's wet hair at the crime scene and witnesses' confirmation of it triggered investigators' suspicion.

Investigators work with firefighters to figure out the cause of a fire.

Where There's Smoke...: The Scene

Smoke Secrets

blue smoke = alcohol-based products

gray-brown smoke = wood, cloth

white smoke = vegetable compounds, phosphorous, hay

yellow/yellow-brown smoke = chemicals, sulfur compounds, gunpowder

black smoke = petroleum products (gasoline, kerosene, etc.)

(Sources: Hidden Evidence by David Owen and The Complete Idiot's Guide to Criminal Investigation by Axelrod and Antinozzi)

Besides obtaining obvious information like where the fire was largest or in what area witnesses first noticed flames, finding out smoke color at different stages during the fire can provide important leads. Alcohol products tend to produce blue smoke, while petroleum-based products yield black smoke. Yellow or yellow-brown smoke is common to chemical fires, including gunpowder and sulfur, while white smoke generally comes from vegetable **compounds**, phosphorous, or hay. Why is smoke color important to know? It can tell investigators if accelerants were present at the start of the blaze, especially if the smoke was black, blue, or yellowish.

Once the squad has facts on which they can intelligently base their next steps, investigators are ready to tackle the rubble. A forensic photographer often accompanies these teams on the first walk-through. Photos and videotapes create a permanent record of the scene as it was immediately after the fire. These images need to be taken before anyone disturbs or removes evidence.

Additionally, some investigators tape comments about what they see on handheld recorders during their walk-through. Others take extensive notes. Either method preserves their initial observations and can jog memories later on, support other evidence, and clarify photographs.

What Do Investigators Look For?

Investigators know that specific materials react to fire in predictable ways but to different degrees, depending on how hot a fire gets and how long it burns. Wood tends to char, paint blisters and peels, glass cracks or melts, stone chips or splits, and metals discolor or liquefy. The varying extent to which fire affects these materials reveals the fire's intensity and duration, but only in the specific area where the material was found.

Understanding fire—what it craves, how it travels, patterns it leaves behind—assists the investigation in many ways. Knowing where a fire burned fast and intensely (or more slowly at lower temperatures) can point investigators toward arson or accident. It can even verify or challenge testimony. In one case, a man claimed he came home to the fire and tried to rescue his wife from their burning bedroom, but he couldn't break down the locked door. If his story was true and the door was closed, the doorjamb facing the hall wouldn't have suffered as much damage as the doorjamb inside the room where the fire was most intense. Blistering patterns on the hallway side of the door said otherwise. When detectives confronted the man with this evidence, proving the door must have been open, the man admitted to being in the room when the fire broke out.

Perhaps the most important use of understanding fire damage comes into play when establishing point of origin. Heat intensity is often greatest at a fire's start, especially if accelerants are involved. So examining post-fire characteristics can determine where a fire originated and how it traveled regardless of what burned (building, car, body, etc.).

Accelerants like gasoline cause smoke to burn black.

CAREER SPOTLIGHT:
Forensic Photographer/
Scene Artist

Forensic photographers and artists preserve the fire scene by shooting it on film from all angles, documenting the locations and conditions of evidence (including bodies) as they're found, and/or diagramming the scene.

Surfaces that burn longer and hotter also burn deeply, so they experience deeper charring. If one area of a fire scene is more deeply charred than other areas, it clearly burned longer; and if it burned longer, the fire must have started there earlier. The area that burned longest and hottest—usually showing the greatest damage—often indicates the fire's point of origin.

Investigators also look for a "V pattern" in burned material to locate a start point. Fires tend to burn up and out, so they often burn walls or other vertical surfaces in the shape of a V. The bottom of the V literally points down to where the fire likely began, so the search for point of origin often begins at the lowest level of the burned-out area.

Finding where a fire originated is critical. It's the foremost challenge of fire investigators once everyone's safe and the fire cooled. If fire investiga-

Hints from a "Trained Eye"

Remember, fire and explosion scenes are notoriously hard to investigate because their events destroy the evidence, but a trained eye can spot signs of arson even in the ashes. Here are a few of those signs:

- Alligatoring—a checkered pattern in charred wood that makes it look like black alligator skin. This pattern means a very hot burn. Small, flat alligatoring indicates longer exposure to intense heat (so it's usually found near the point of origin) while large, bubbly alligatoring indicates rapid, intense heat.
- Crazing—intricate, web-like cracks throughout glass. Extensive crazing can indicate rapid and intense heat that, in turn, indicates accelerant use. However, crazing can also happen when cold water—like that from firefighters' hoses—hits hot glass of 500°F (260°C) or more, so crazing can indicate accelerants, but doesn't necessarily guarantee it.
- Line of demarcation—an abrupt line between charred and less charred (or even uncharred) surfaces. Such a line, especially if puddle shaped, is definitely suspicious and can indicate accelerant use.
- Spalling—breaking off (chipping and flaking, not splitting) of surface pieces of stone, brick, or concrete. Intense heat is required to trigger spalling, and brown stains around a spall area can indicate accelerant use.

If accelerants are present, the possibility of arson increases.

tors can determine where a fire started, they can begin to focus on how it started. That's when they look even more closely at the fire's remains and start identifying, collecting, and preserving even the tiniest piece of evidence.

Too Hot
to Handle:
The Evidence

"I have to hunt. I have to search. There's always a step, step, step."
—Jack Carney, a retired fire investigator, from *Catching Fire* by Gena K. Gorrell

Collecting evidence at a fire scene is tricky business. Though it certainly requires visually examining and chronicling the scene, documentation doesn't end there. Evidence collectors must carefully gather, contain, label, and log every bit of potential evidence in detail. It's painstaking work.

Packaging and Transporting Evidence

Members of the investigating team first record each location where they find evidence using written notes, sketches, and photo or video journals, and then they enter that documentation into an evidence recovery log. Next, they physically gather the evidence. This step is delicate. Anyone who handles potential evidence must be extremely careful not to damage or contaminate it. Everyone who gathers evidence must wear sterile, disposable gloves—just like on TV, except that most real-life handlers use fresh gloves for each item.

Some investigators use disposable tools to avoid cross-contamination (getting material from one area of the fire scene mixed with evidence from another area). Throwaways range from long, sterile swabs that look like Q-tips to tweezers, from putty knives to spades. Each find is placed in a clean, unused, airtight container—for example, a glass jar, laboratory-approved bag, or metal can—so investigators can safely transport the evidence to the lab.

Meanwhile, Back in Kansas

From witness interviews, Johnson County fire officials knew the house had become engulfed in flames so quickly that they had to consider arson. They also realized an accelerant must have been present because of the large amount of black smoke. Additionally, they knew two children hadn't made it out of the Prairie Village blaze. Facts from initial interviews helped them know what they were looking for.

The coroner's office (or medical examiner's office depending on locale) pronounces death, removes bodies, and orders or performs forensic

CAREER SPOTLIGHT:
Medical Examiner/ Coroner/ Forensic Pathologist

Medical Examiner: A licensed physician (licensed to practice medicine and trained in forensic pathology) who performs autopsies and investigates any unattended deaths and all deaths by violence, suicide, or criminal acts.

Coroner: An appointed or elected official (formerly requiring no medical or forensic skills, but more and more requiring a medical background) who takes charge of corpses and can order autopsies.

Forensic Pathologist: A licensed physician trained in pathology (diseases and injuries and the functional or structural changes they cause in the human body); is in charge of evidentiary corpses and all evidence gathered from examining them; conducts autopsies; pursues answers using medical records, interviews, and lab evidence.

autopsies. In this case, once the children's bodies were found, the coroner's office gathered and transported them, and the assistant coroner did the autopsies. She found that both children died from smoke inhalation, just as investigators thought. Neither child showed any wounds other than those from the smoke and fire. Conclusion: each child had been alive when the fire erupted. It proves the fire wasn't set to cover their murders; fire was the murder weapon.

Once the county fire marshal suspected both arson and murder, he activated his task force. This group included personnel from Johnson County's Fire District No. 2, other local fire units, local law enforcement agencies, the three-county Eastern Kansas Multi-Agency Task Force, the Kansas Bureau of Investigation (KBI), the ATF, and the International Association of Arson Investigators (IAAI).

They began in the basement because accidental fires often start there. After ruling out causes like the two water heaters, two furnaces, two electrical panels, and utility lines, they came to a basement fitness room. Here, they could look through the ceiling, through the living room above, all the way to the *joists*. But surprisingly, the fire hadn't started on this lowest level; scorching patterns showed flames had begun to burn downward into this floor after running out of fuel in the living room. Forensic photographers didn't overlook the inverted burn patterns. The room was virtually untouched except for the damaged ceiling.

The rest of the basement level also remained remarkably clean, but one investigator stumbled upon a book on the floor near a wet bar on that level. Heat had seared its edges, but the book remained intact: Nobody Gets Out of Here Alive. He bagged it, labeled it, and initialed the find. Prosecutors later used it as evidence against Green to show that she planned, even researched, her crime.

Deadly Elements

There are four parts to every fire. All of them are dangerous.

Fire Gas: Invisible gases the burning process produces. Many of them, like carbon monoxide, are toxic to humans. Many fire victims die of carbon monoxide poisoning from breathing these gases long before fire reaches them.

Flame: The colored light (blue, green, orange, yellow, white) produced by burning gases. Color varies with what is burning.

Heat: The part of fire that you can feel. Technically it is heat, not the light of flames, that burns your skin. A typical fire reaches 1,100°F (593°C). We usually bake chicken at around 350° to 400°F (177° to 204°C). Triple that, and you get an idea of heat's power to injure or kill.

Smoke: Clouds of vapor mixed with extremely fine particles of what's burning. Many people die from inhaling smoke, which damages the lungs.

(Source: Fire! by Joy Masoff)

Discerning Detection

Keep in mind that anything an investigator thinks might have evidentiary value is fair game at this point—from dust, ashes, and the tiniest shattered glass to bodies, structural beams, and entire cars. Other forensic processes later determine its real value. A microscopic plastic fragment could be a remnant of a pipe bomb; a splice of wire, a timing device; or a strip of

A Molotov cocktail can cause a sudden, but devastating explosion.

cloth, the fuse of a **Molotov cocktail**. At this stage of the investigation, the investigators just don't know.

Where evidence is found can be extremely telling; so can its condition. For example, clean slivers of glass far away from a fire's center could indicate the fire began from an explosion. Conversely, smoky splinters of glass near the fire's point of origin could suggest fire set off an explosion.

Metals, too, can provide insights based on their condition and location. Brass melts at 1724°F (940°C), and aluminum melts at 1220°F (660°C). If the aluminum bottom of a pan melted but its brass handle didn't, the fire where the pan was must have reached temperatures of at least 1220°F but below 1724°F. Knowing how hot a fire got where and when helps direct detectives to point of origin and can suggest the presence of accelerants.

Even something as simple as a stopped watch can be important. It might reveal the time fire reached its location, or its battery could have died months ago! Investigators won't know unless they collect and examine it.

In rare cases, determining a fire's point of origin, cause, and timetable requires virtually no detection at all. However, it still requires solid confirmation. A 2005 firebombing in Hamilton, Ontario, is a good example.

At 3:40 a.m. on Sunday, February 6, witnesses observed a masked man running from a bar, then around the corner, just before hearing a car speed away. First they saw him throw what looked like a Molotov cocktail into the building. Then they watched him bolt. The immediate explosion was powerful enough to throw glass across the street. (Clean glass. Far away from fire central.) Fire crews raced to the bar but not in time to prevent the resulting blaze from gutting the business. From strictly a detection point of view, it didn't really matter; fire investigators had time, point of origin, and cause from witness interviews. Their search for evidence in the rubble simply confirmed all three.

CAREER SPOTLIGHT:
Crime Scene Investigators (CSIs)

These investigators locate, collect, and protect physical evidence at a crime scene, whether the crime is arson, murder, assault, rape, or robbery. They also transport all evidence to a crime lab. They train to see and handle evidence, including spotting, recognizing, collecting, preserving, and transporting it, but they don't usually perform actual lab tests. Different communities require different qualifications for CSIs, from certification to advanced degrees.

From shards of glass to charred carpet, the amount of potential evidence in any fire or explosion can clearly be staggering, regardless of how it's used. It can take weeks, months, or years to process an entire scene. Fire detectives only find what they're looking for by literally digging through tons of ruins one layer at a time. Whether to detect or confirm facts in the case, there's no way around this painstaking process.

The Johnson County team moved upstairs to the house's ground floor. There it found extensive damage, but not enough to cover arson's tracks. The front foyer's floor had been tile; the stairwell leading from it to the kids' rooms upstairs was carpeted. Pour patterns—stark edges that mark an unnatural meeting of cooler and hot burns such as those left where accelerants do and do not land—covered floor surfaces in both areas.

Accelerants will burn hottest where they are poured, leaving a trail of evidence for investigators to find.

Flammable liquid had soaked the carpeted stairs so thoroughly that flames "rolled" under the carpet tread to burn each riser, some all the way through. The landing at the top of the steps was just as bad. Anyone upstairs when the fire was set would have been trapped instantly. But the team needed to prove what it saw.

Investigators cut identical carpet and tile samples from three separate areas to compare: badly burned, less burned, and unburned. (The unburned, or "clean," sample is the **control sample**.) They carefully placed each one into separate evidence containers and sealed them. Because the evidence—accelerants on carpet—could evaporate, the investigators placed the samples in airtight cans. The investigators wanted the lab to test these carpet and floor swatches for flammable liquids. That process could take weeks, even months, but in evidence cans, the samples would be safe. No one was allowed to break their seals until forensic technicians in the lab opened each specimen to run tests.

The breakfast area and closet immediately below one of the children's rooms had the same pour patterns as the front foyer, and similar isolated and uneven charring scarred every room like a path leading to the mother's room. Furthermore, investigators found a thin, clean strip of carpet the size of the bottom end of Green's door angling away from the door frame. That spot proved her bedroom door was open during the fire; it had protected the carpet underneath. Photographers documented every detail.

Someone had clearly poured accelerants throughout the house, starting with the upstairs hall, pouring more heavily down the steps, into the foyer, and onto ground-floor surfaces beneath each child's room, then finally backward to the master suite. The burn level and amount of accelerant in these areas indicated multiple points of origin. This fire was intentional, and it seemed directed at the children.

CAREER SPOTLIGHT:
Crime Scene Investigators

Latent Print Examiners: Specialists who uncover, obtain, and examine fingerprints, footprints, and palm prints and then compare them to print databases or other records. This includes any found at an arson scene.

Dactyloscopists: Specialists who analyze and compare fingerprints.

Room by room, layer by layer, fire inspectors continued their examination of the scene. Detectives also found at least one, empty, lighter-fluid bottle in the garage area. They bagged that, too, and sent it to the lab. Green's fingerprints were all over it.

Many arsonists assume fire destroys all fingerprints. Though fire destroys many of them, prints in blood, soft paint, window putty, and so on may remain after exposure to heat. Anything that softens in a fire—like a plastic lighter-fluid bottle—can take on fingerprint impressions and survive.

Preserving Evidence

Once a container is sealed, the person who gathered its contents—a police officer, a firefighter, or another official scene investigator—labels it clearly and uniquely to avoid any later confusion or mix-up. Labeling includes the case number, the name of the collector (each must initial her own finds), the date and time of collection, the location at which she gathered the sample, a specimen number, and a description of what's in the container. It's crucial that every collector package everything personally and according to laboratory requirements.

Perhaps the two most important challenges in the evidence-gathering process are preventing any changes in the condition of the evidence once it's collected (contamination) and maintaining its "chain of custody." Chain of custody is simply a continuous record (without any gaps even minutes long) showing that officials kept the evidence intact and accounted for along every step of the process—from the fire scene to the lab and ultimately to the courtroom. That journey can take years, so each person who handles evidence at any point must sign that he did so. Evidence is worth-

Chain of Custody

No single person handles a piece of evidence from fire scene to courtroom. Each and every individual who handles it along the way must initial or sign for it and date the container in which it's preserved. That person is then responsible for maintaining the integrity of the evidence (keeping it undamaged, uncompromised, "as is") until he or she passes it along to the next person in the chain. Here's how this process generally works:

1. The person who finds, packages, and labels the evidence signs it over to one of the fire-scene investigators at the scene. This person can be a police officer, fire official, crime-scene technician, investigator, or anyone else officially examining the fire scene.

2. That investigator then transports the evidence to the lab and signs it over to a lab technician.

3. Once tests are complete, that lab technician signs the evidence over to an officer in charge of the police department's evidence storage area. That officer is the "custodian of evidence."

4. The custodian of evidence locks up the evidence in the storage area until someone needs it again. (If, for example, the district attorney's office needs to run additional chemical tests on a gasoline-soaked rag from an arson scene, it must sign the rag both out and back in again. The rag must be signed in and out of the lab again, too.)

5. The evidence remains in police custody until the prosecuting attorney signs it out to present in court.

less if the chain of custody is broken or if the sample becomes tainted or damaged. Either failure renders evidence inadmissible in court.

The chain of custody never broke for carpet and tile samples investigators collected at the Green house. It remained secure, too, for the hair specimen police took that night, the book, and the lighter-fluid bottle. No one could question this evidence's integrity. And not only did a forensic chemist find that fire did indeed scorch a number of Green's hairs on the front and sides of her head, lab technicians also found isoparaffins (a common ingredient in lighter fluid) in the most heavily fire-damaged carpet and floor samples. In fact, saturation levels indicated the arsonist used between three and ten gallons of flammable liquids to start the blaze. Whoever started the fire clearly meant business.

CAREER SPOTLIGHT:
Forensic Chemist

Forensic chemists examine the molecular attributes of solid and liquid evidence like glass, stone, wood, metal, paint, dyes, chemicals, fibers, and even ashes. They analyze the molecular makeup of such substances using techniques that can range from liquid chemical tests to visual comparisons under a scanning electron microscope. In arson cases, investigators often depend on forensic chemists to verify or exclude the presence of accelerants in samples taken from the scene. A college degree is required.

Lab Locale

Most of the hundreds of pieces of evidence gathered at any arson scene require additional scientific testing to confirm or exclude their value as evidence. That's where the forensic lab (or criminalistics lab) comes in.

Canada

The RCMP operates a system of forensic labs across the country. Additionally, city and provincial laboratories are located in Vancouver, Montreal, and Ottawa.

United States

Nationally, the FBI and ATF operate well-respected forensic labs at multiple locations. Additionally, and perhaps more practically, most states have at least one state criminalistics lab, which can provide most of the testing a fire investigator would ever need. Some larger states even have a system of regional labs to reduce costs and travel time.

Accelerants shout arson when traces of them end up in household areas where most people wouldn't use flammable liquids, especially in large quantities. Accelerant residue on a couch, bed, or, as in this case, all over a stairwell simply isn't explainable with normal living habits. (Traces of gasoline on a garage floor could be.) And, unless the fire is unusually hot, most accelerants don't completely burn. Forensic chemistry generally finds it. In fact, forensic chemistry might possibly be the most important lab aspect (as opposed to site observation) of distinguishing arson from accidents.

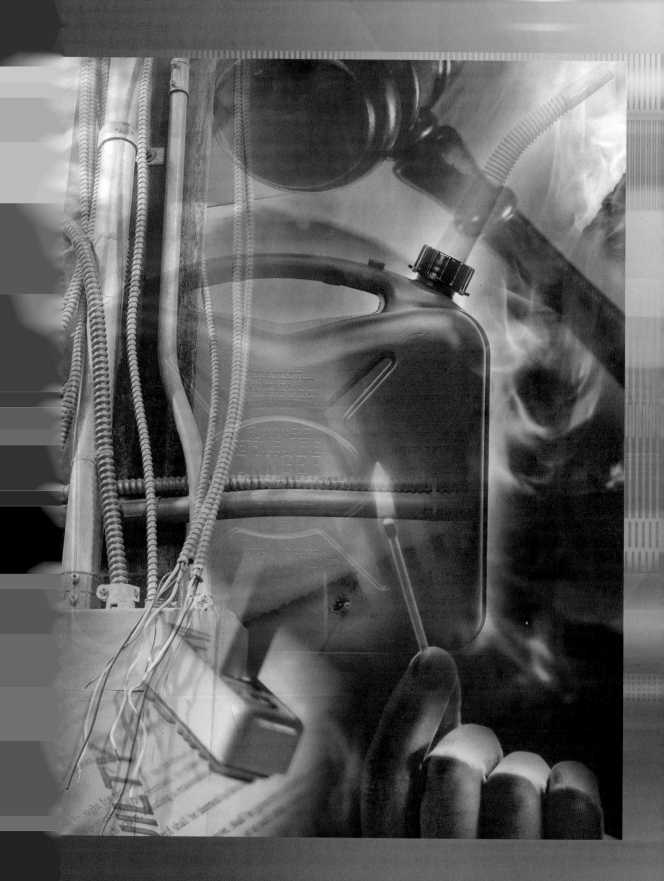

4

Burning Questions: Accident or Crime?

"I am an innocent man, convicted of a crime I did not commit. I have been persecuted for twelve years for something I did not do." These are among the last words of Cameron Todd Willingham before he was executed by the State of Texas on February 17, 2003, for the 1991 arson-murders of his three daughters. He protested his innocence to the end.

At least one Cambridge University chemist, a Ph.D. and renowned fire scientist, believed him. Was it an accidental fire or arson?

During the original investigation of the 1991 house fire, investigators concluded that Willingham had used an accelerant to set three separate fires inside his one-story, wood-frame home. They based their conclusions on traditional "visual" fire knowledge: crazed glass, floor-burn patterns, and wood charring. In some cases, such conditions are unquestionably signs of arson; in this case, they may not have been.

For example, every expert at the time agreed that this fire did reach the point of flashover. Flashover happens when air (gas) in a room builds up and becomes so hot that everything in the room bursts into flames at the same time, causing a massive explosion; fire engulfs the entire room. Fifteen years later, experts now know that once flashover happens, it's virtually impossible to visually identify pour patterns. (Today, labs can confirm or exclude the presence of accelerants through laboratory analysis.) Yet it was the visual identification alone of these patterns (without lab verification) that helped convict Willingham.

Fire experts in 1991 also testified that accelerants caused the charring scars they found under an aluminum threshold at the house. Yet liquid accelerants can't burn under aluminum (or any closed area) anymore than a candle can burn in a sealed jar. Both require oxygen.

Last, what about the crazing? In 1991, it was thought that crazing automatically indicated an accelerant fire because of the intense heat required to crack glass. Fire experts didn't know any other cause for crazing. The National Fire Protection Association (NFPA) didn't release until February 1992 its studies showing that spraying hot glass with cooler water—as when firefighters spray a fire—can also cause crazing.

"At the time of the fire, we were still testifying to things we know aren't accurate today," admitted one deputy fire marshal who assisted in the original investigation. "They were true then, but they aren't now."

A contemporary expert agreed. "There is nothing to suggest to any reasonable arson investigator [today] that this was an arson fire," asserted Gerald Hurst, a Cambridge University chemist and fire investigator. "It was just a fire." His objections came too late for Cameron Todd Willingham.

Accurately distinguishing accidents from arson is obviously vital for all concerned. The task is no less critical with explosions, and neither arena is simple. Some claim interpreting fire evidence is more art than science; others say more science than art. The problem with both fires and explosions—whether accidental or deliberate—is that by their very nature, they destroy evidence. By definition, they self-destruct.

According to InterFIRE, arson is the least often investigated and least prosecuted criminal offense in America. Why? The overwhelming majority of evidence in arson and bombing cases is circumstantial. Witnesses are rare; the "smoking gun" is nearly nonexistent. And circumstantial cases are the hardest criminal cases to prove in court. Many potential arson and bombing prosecutions never make it there; prosecutors often reject them for

Arson can rarely be proven.

Burning Questions: Accident or Crime?

Fast Fact:
Fire Classifications

Regarding origin (cause), every fire incident falls into one of five, general, official classifications:

- natural (lightning, etc.)
- accidental (faulty wiring, cigarette in bed, cooking, playing with matches, etc.)
- unknown origin (investigators are unable to determine what happened)
- suspicious (some indications of arson, but not enough to be certain)
- incendiary (obvious arson)

"insufficient evidence." But is typical arson/bombing evidence really insufficient? To satisfy a legal standard, maybe it is; to satisfy common sense, maybe not.

Arson Fires and Bombings

Fires and explosions are actually very similar. Both are reactions to combining oxygen, fuel, and an ignition source. In fact, fires often lead to secondary explosions, and explosions often lead to secondary fires. The main difference separating the two is their reaction rates. Explosions consume fuel nearly instantaneously, whereas fires consume their fuel more gradually.

Because they are so similar, investigating a bomb scene requires the same level of attention as searching a fire scene, and many of the same approaches apply. As discussed in previous chapters, the first step in any fire event is to establish point of origin, then cause. That's also true of bombings.

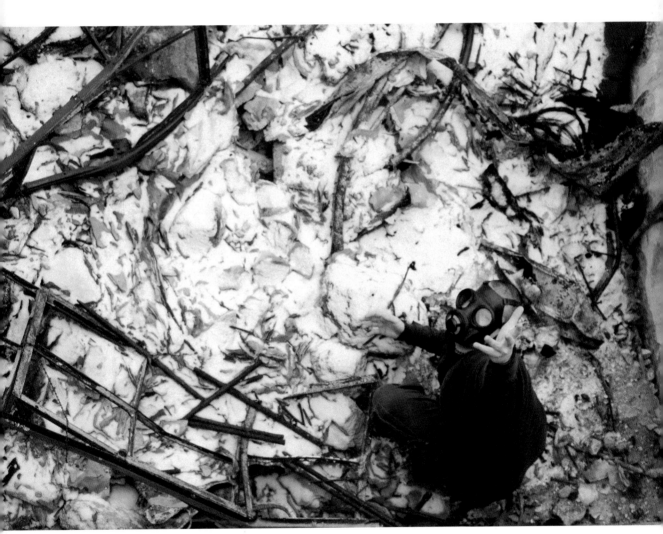

An investigator scours a bomb site for clues.

Burning Questions: Accident or Crime? 69

Intriguing Indicators

Arson

When a fire is intentional, it boasts very specific characteristics:

- The fire burns faster, larger, and hotter than accidental and natural fires.
- It often has multiple points of origin.
- Suspicious cans or containers are sometimes nearby.
- Unnatural concentrations of accelerants are present, even if only in trace amounts. (Accelerants can be liquid as in gasoline or solid like a stack of paper or furniture.)
- A time-delay device is often in the rubble. (Time-delay devices include items as simple as a matchbook or cigarette. Some cigarettes provide up to twenty-two minutes of "fuse" time.)

Bombs

When a fire is the result of a bombing, it, too, leaves very specific clues:

- A bomb almost always leaves a crater. The size (diameter and depth) depends on the power of the explosion.
- The center of the crater is the obvious and single point of origin (unless multiple bombs were set off).

- Explosives residue is common on fragments radiating from ground zero.
- Evidence of timers or other delay devices (like battery fragments, wire, or switches) is often in the rubble.
- Evidence of a bomb's container (like bottle fragments, pipe segments, end caps, and even shards of radios, computers, or other electronic equipment in which bombers commonly hide their devices) often survives the explosion/blaze. The tiniest piece can still hold partial fingerprints.

Once investigators have ruled out accidental and natural triggers for either a fire or explosion and determined that its start was at least "suspicious," the real investigation begins. How can investigators initially tell if a fire or explosion was deliberate? Arson and bombings both leave distinct trails.

By far, the most common indicator of arson and bombings is the presence of trace amounts of accelerants or explosives. Fire investigators study the distinct marks they leave behind and can usually spot them in the most charred ruins. But occasionally, all visible traces of accelerants burn in a blaze. What can detectives do then if they still suspect arson? Where should they begin to look if they can't see any clues? In many cases, that's when K-9 units go to work.

Accelerant-Detecting Canines

"Arson dogs" train much like dogs that sniff out drugs or people trapped underneath earthquake rubble or a child lost in the wilderness. All these dogs learn to react to specific scents, only instead of human or narcotic scents, arson dogs are trained to react to those of flammable substances and other accelerants. Rescue workers and law enforcement officers have long recognized the power of a dog's nose. If dogs can detect drugs and people, why not use them to detect arson?

A cooperative effort of national, state, and local agencies in New Haven, Connecticut, launched the first accelerant-detection K-9 training program in 1985. (Dozens of such programs are now operating all over the United States and Canada.) Developers built their program around the idea that dogs could narrow a fire-scene search area by honing in on suspicious debris when they sensed specific accelerants. The dogs, of course, couldn't say what the substance was, just that it was there. Then investigators could gather samples from those locations and submit them for lab analysis.

The last part of that last sentence is key. Yes, arson dogs can show detectives where to look, but the lab tells them if they're right and what the accelerant is. Both dog and lab are necessary to the process.

"He who uses the dog as an expert without lab confirmation is a fool," states Sergeant Jeff Howard, then arson section manager with the Oregon State Police (OSP), in the 1997 article "Arson Dogs" by Kelly Andersson. "The dog is just a tool." Some investigators believe it's an invaluable one.

Accelerant-detecting canines can find traces so small they escape electronic detection. One independent study showed dogs can detect half-evaporated gasoline in quantities as small as .01 microliter (or about 1/1000 of a drop) 100 percent of the time. They can also alert investigators to the strongest concentrations of accelerants, not just where an accelerant is. That's

CAREER SPOTLIGHT:
Arson Dog Handler

When detectives suspect arson, they sometimes bring in specially trained "accelerant-detecting dogs" to sniff out traces of accelerants and explosives in fire debris. (Some can also find bodies.) Each dog has a handler with whom it resides. The handler cares for and trains with the dog, then accompanies it on all investigations. Occasionally, dog–person teams travel across the country to assist in the investigation of large fires, explosions, or other disasters.

important, particularly when someone throws gasoline all over a room. The percentage of "positive" accelerant-detection results at some labs nearly doubled once K-9 units went to work.

Other Accelerant-
Detecting Devices

Beside dogs, another tool for detecting accelerants at a fire scene is the vapor trace analyzer (VTA). This portable device is an extremely sensitive "gas chromatograph" that can be used to test for hydrocarbon traces in the air surrounding potential accelerant residue. Most arsonists use petroleum-based, highly flammable hydrocarbons like gasoline. A VTA reacts to hydrocarbons.

Every VTA has three main parts: a nozzle, heating element, and temperature gauge. The operator draws an air sample from around suspicious debris into the VTA through its nozzle, like a gentle vacuum. The sample passes over the heating element inside. If an air sample burns when it encounters the heating element, hydrocarbons must be present. Their burning raises the temperature in the VTA, which in turn causes its temperature gauge to rise. Any jump in the temperature gauge tells the operator flammable residue is present. Then investigators take solid samples from the area where the VTA reacted and submit them for lab analysis.

Some police dogs are trained to sniff out explosive materials.

Isolating the Culprits

The most common methods for separating then isolating suspected accelerants from their samples are:

- headspace vapor extraction: Testers place the fire-scene specimen in a closed container and heat it. Any hydrocarbon residue will create a vapor-rich gas in the air-filled space above the material. Lab analysts remove the vapor with a syringe and test it for hydrocarbons.
- steam distillation: Lab technicians heat a charred sample and collect and condense any steam it gives off. The resulting liquid is then tested for hydrocarbons.
- solvent extraction: Testers place the fire-scene sample in a container with a solvent. The solvent dissolves the sample material (carpet, wood, etc.) leaving behind any residual hydrocarbons, which are then extracted and tested.
- vapor concentration: Testers heat the fire-scene sample in a closed container with charcoal. Charcoal absorbs any hydrocarbons the sample gives off during the heating process. Testers then extract the hydrocarbons from the charcoal using a solvent. (This method was first borrowed from air pollution scientists and then perfected by an ATF chemist.)

(Sources: Crime Lab: A Guide for Nonscientists by John Houde and Forensics for Dummies by D. P. Lyle, M.D.)

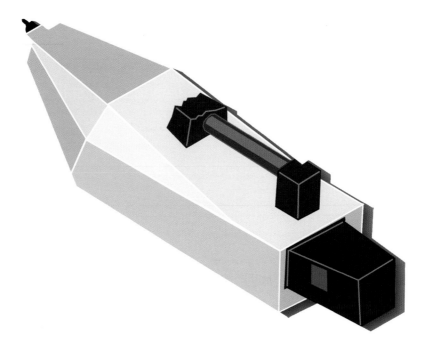

A portable explosive trace detector

Lab Magic

Once a sample reaches the lab, the first step is to separate and isolate the potential accelerant (a compound) from the sample. Lab technicians have a number of methods they can use to single out these questionable compounds. After lab personnel isolate their chemical suspects, they generally use one of three methods to identify them: gas chromatography, mass spectroscopy, or infrared spectrophotometry. The first two are the most common procedures.

Gas chromatography (GC) relies on the fact that scientists can identify compounds by knowing how far each part of the compound moves through a "carrier gas" and how quickly. Here's how it works: A technician injects a liquid sample of the compound into the end of a column where it's heated. The liquid gradually vaporizes and enters the tube, flowing with a moving carrier gas toward a detector. The compound's different ingredients—now in vapor form—move with the carrier gas at different speeds, and some fall behind while others pull ahead. Simply put, they separate. As the carrier gas passes over the detector, the detector picks up each component in the gas and signals a plotting device that records it on a continuous line graph.

Peaks and valleys along the line graph indicate when and how much of the respective ingredients passed through. A peak shows the amount of a component, and the distance left to right shows how long that component took to pass through the tube. This graph is called a chromatograph. GC

Studies conducted in the lab may turn up conclusive evidence in a crime.

Burning Questions: Accident or Crime?

is so accurate it can distinguish brands of gasoline, let alone gasoline from other accelerants.

In more cases than not, GC is sufficient to determine what an unknown sample from a fire scene is. Occasionally, lab technicians will combine GC with mass spectroscopy (MS) just to be sure. MS literally shatters the compound by bombarding it with a beam of high-energy electrons. These fragments then pass over a magnetic or electric field that attracts them individually by mass. Technicians compare the pattern the fragments make (the unknown pattern) to known fragmentation patterns, hoping to find a match. If they do, they can identify the substance.

When technicians combine GC and MS, the combination test is called a gas chromatograph-mass spectrometer (GC-MS). The GC feeds each gaseous compound it separated directly into the MS; the MS further fragments that compound and identifies its respective masses. Lab technicians can isolate and name virtually any compound by combining these two processes.

GC and MS are the main methods labs use to confirm or exclude any presence of suspect substances in fire-scene samples. The procedures may seem like magic, but the results are measurable, objective, and scientific. Arson detectives know that. By far, the most frequently requested testing fire and explosion investigators ask labs to perform is for accelerants and explosives. They're the most common ingredients in intentional destruction.

Seeing the Whole Picture

The mere presence of an accelerant or explosive does not automatically mean a fire or explosion was set deliberately. For example, a person might have spilled gasoline on his garage floor and then inadvertently set it ablaze when he flicked ashes from a cigarette. Or another person could

CAREER SPOTLIGHT:

Lab Technicians

Various specialists handle defined areas of laboratory analysis (like chromatography). They learn technology unique to their specialty and apply it in a laboratory setting. Qualifications range from certification in a specific process to advanced general degrees, depending on the specialty.

Trace Evidence Examiners

These specialists analyze and compare fibers, soils, paints, hair, or any other trace evidence to determine its type and origin.

have mistakenly poured gasoline in a kerosene heater and triggered an explosion. The presence of accelerants or explosives merely tells investigators to dig deeper. Answering questions of motive, potential gain, and opportunity helps them do that.

On the morning of July 9, 1985, Steven Benson arrived at his grandmother's home to pick up some things he needed. Just before 9:00 a.m., he, his mother, brother, and sister headed back out to the car to run some errands. Saying he forgot something, Steven threw his keys to his brother and went back into the house. When Steven's brother climbed in and turned on the ignition, the car blew. Other than Steven, the only survivor was his sister. His mother and brother died in the explosion.

Burning Questions: Accident or Crime?

When the first investigators arrived, they noted Steven seemed abnormally calm for someone who had just lost his mother and brother so violently, and for someone who had just narrowly escaped death himself. That was their first clue. (Interview information)

Suspicion grew when they searched the wreckage. The forensic investigators discovered pieces of four 1.5-volt batteries and parts of a circuit board and switch that didn't belong to the car. They also found obvious bomb fragments: a steel pipe and two end-caps. (Physical evidence from the scene)

Additional investigative work over subsequent weeks revealed Benson stood to inherit a large sum of money—$10 million—if his elder family members died. Furthermore, he had been stealing from his mother for quite some time, and she'd just found out. She was about to change her will—to exclude him—right before the explosion. (Motive: monetary gain)

Six weeks and one day after the car bombing, police arrested Steven Benson. Nearly one year later, a jury found him guilty of the murders of his mother and brother.

Notice that all the evidence against Benson was circumstantial, but that doesn't mean its parts were unscientific or weak. Neither investigators nor the accused questioned if the explosion was a car bombing or if it was a deliberate act. Solid, objective, lab-verified, physical evidence eradicated any thought of an accidental explosion. Detectives moved on to why and who.

No one saw Steven make or plant the bomb. No one saw him set it off. But strong bomb-scene evidence, interviews, the defendant's behavior immediately before and after the explosion, other physical evidence (personal receipts for the bomb parts), and the "money trail" collectively pointed to only one suspect. The jury agreed.

A Joint Effort

Even if an incident is clearly an arson or bombing, as it was in the Benson case, occasionally its author is clever enough to avoid suspicion. Then typical investigative procedures don't produce any suspects. In such cases, additional forensic specialties can help. This scenario is particularly true of random crimes.

Consider the Unabomber, Ted Kaczynski, who killed and injured over twenty people with homemade bombs. His writing style, not crime-scene evidence, eventually gave him away. David Kaczynski, Ted's brother, recognized the wording of a 35,000-word manifesto the *New York Times* and

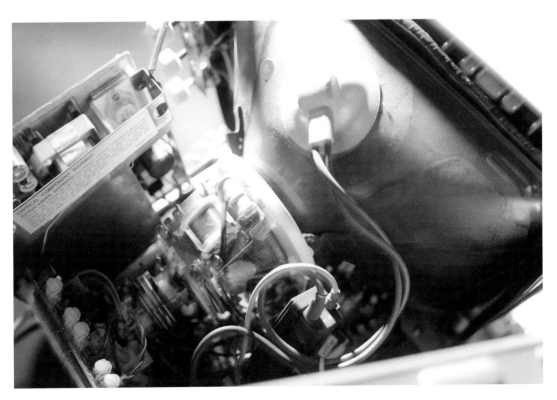

The remnants of a bomb were found in the exploded car.

Washington Post jointly published in response to the serial bomber's promise to stop his attacks. Desperate for leads after seventeen years, fifteen bombings, twenty-two injuries, and three deaths, federal investigators allowed the essay's release. It worked.

Using control samples for comparison—unrelated specimens of Ted's work, which David provided—a forensic linguist (words), a forensic document examiner (general authenticity), and a forensic graphologist (handwriting) each analyzed the original manifesto. They unanimously agreed that the same mind and hand created Ted's control samples and the Unabomber's lengthy treatise. Ted Kaczynski and the Unabomber were the same man.

Did investigators know the explosions weren't accidents? Yes. Did they find physical evidence at each of the fifteen bomb scenes? Certainly, but

An abundance of incriminating evidence led the jury to convict Steven Benson.

CAREER SPOTLIGHT:

Handwriting, Linguistics, and Document Analysis

Many serial arsonists and bombers crave the notoriety their crimes give them. One way to assure they'll get attention is with letters to the media. Here are a few forensic careers that examine such written evidence:

- Forensic Document Examiner: Examines written and printed materials to identify and/or confirm how old the material is, its authorship, and its authenticity.
- Forensic Graphologist: Examines and compares handwriting samples to prove or disprove someone wrote or signed a specific document.
- Forensic Linguist: Evaluates speaking and writing styles including vocabulary, word selection, sentence structure, phraseology, and so on, to assist in profiling or identifying a suspect, crime pattern, or motive.

without a person to whom they could connect it, let alone any motive, the evidence sat unused for years. Language and writing experts (with the help of the Kaczynski family) provided that critical link.

The Unabomber case involved many small incidents over multiple years, yet cooperation among various forensic disciplines ultimately solved those crimes. Imagine the teamwork that comes into play when you have a bomb-

To solve an arson case, investigators must use teamwork.

EXPLOSIVES & ARSON INVESTIGATION

ing the size of the Oklahoma City bombing or the events of September 11, 2001. Incidents like these present huge challenges to investigators: sheer size of search areas, debris volume, scores of people to interview, and numerous bodies to recover, assess, and identify. Gathering and coordinating staff alone can be daunting. Clearly, in less obvious cases of such magnitude, determining "accident" or "incendiary" might take a very long time. Yet the basic approach to gathering forensic evidence remains the same regardless of scale.

Death Tolls

Many cases of arson and bombing don't involve any loss of life. In fact, most arson cases are about insurance money or destroying evidence, not physical harm. Therefore, just like with accelerants, the mere presence of a body at a fire scene or explosion does not itself indicate either intent or innocent accident.

Furthermore, many people mistakenly believe that if a body is found curled tight in the fetal position (pugilistic position), it proves the victim was alive when fire reached him. That's simply not true. During a fire, intense heating dehydrates a body—even dead ones—causing all the muscles to contract. Arms and legs flex more and more as the body dehydrates, and its fists eventually tuck beneath the chin, much like a boxer. If investigators come upon charred bodies in this stance, they know the fire was hot and long, but precisely nothing about whether it was accidental or if the victim was even alive at the time of the fire.

Where a victim dies, the condition of the body, its position in the room, and the state of items surrounding it tell investigators far more. In one of the cases at the beginning of chapter 1, detectives came upon a young woman's charred corpse lying on its side in the middle of an unlit, unheated

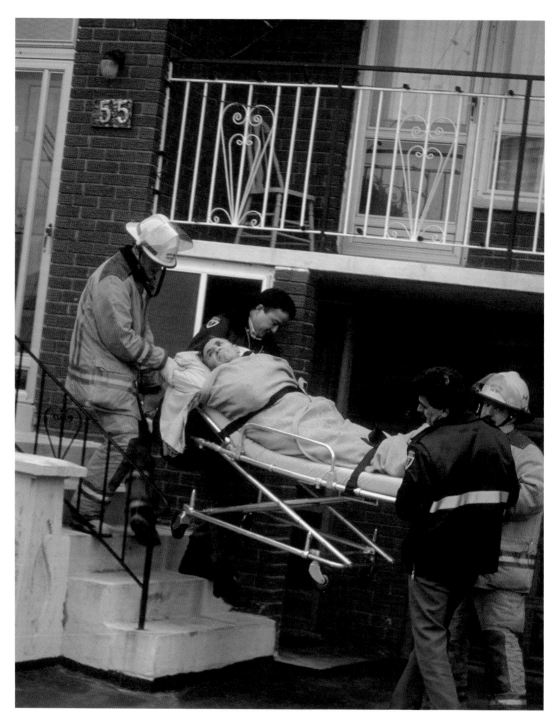

Firefighters remove a victim from the scene of a fire.

Misguided Murderers

Cremating a human body minimally requires sustained 1500°F (815°C) temperatures for at least two hours. Even that kind of exposure leaves ash and bone residue. Killers who try to cover their tracks by setting bodies on fire obviously skipped "Mortuary Science 101." Most accelerant fires, particularly structural ones, burn neither long enough nor hot enough to completely destroy a human body. Structural fires typically range from 500° to 2000°F (260° to 1100°C) over the course of the blaze, but they don't sustain those highest temperatures for long. Therefore, most body and structural fires will not likely accomplish what the murderer-arsonist sets out to do.

basement. When they found the body, it was still in the sitting position in which it had been tied. Traces of duct tape clung to the woman's ankles and wrists.

Fire investigators noticed the greatest fire damage centered on the victim, particularly her head, upper body, and hands. She was the point of origin. Pour patterns on the floor around her indicated accelerants. Clearly, someone had tied up this woman; clearly, someone had held her captive in that basement, and clearly, someone had tried to prevent anyone from discovering who she was. It was obvious to investigators that the fire was not accidental.

CAREER SPOTLIGHT:

Forensic Odontologist

A forensic dentist identifies victims who cannot otherwise be identified by comparing dental records to a body's teeth; he or she can also analyze and compare bite-mark wounds to a suspect's teeth. This career requires an advanced degree in dentistry.

Forensic Anthropologist

This specialist studies human bones to determine the identity of the deceased (gender, age, race, etc.); he or she also examines the circumstances in which the bones were found and may consult on time-of-death issues. The career requires an advanced degree in physical anthropology.

A group of kidnappers set this victim on fire to cover up their role in what they thought was her accidental death (she was actually still barely alive) and to destroy any means of identifying her body. They poured gasoline all over her and around the chair to which she was taped. Then they set it ablaze, hoping intense fire would consume her face and hands, thereby making visual or fingerprint identification impossible. It did, but these kidnappers-turned-murderers also fell prey to a common myth that

Fire personnel must be wary of looming dangers—like backdraft—while investigating a fire.

Burning Questions: Accident or Crime?

accelerant fires burn long enough and hot enough to completely destroy a body. They don't.

Out of the Ashes

When fires or bombs do take a life, they often do so more completely than other causes of death. Injuries they impose sometimes rob victims of their identities. Forensic anthropology and forensic odontology can counter this.

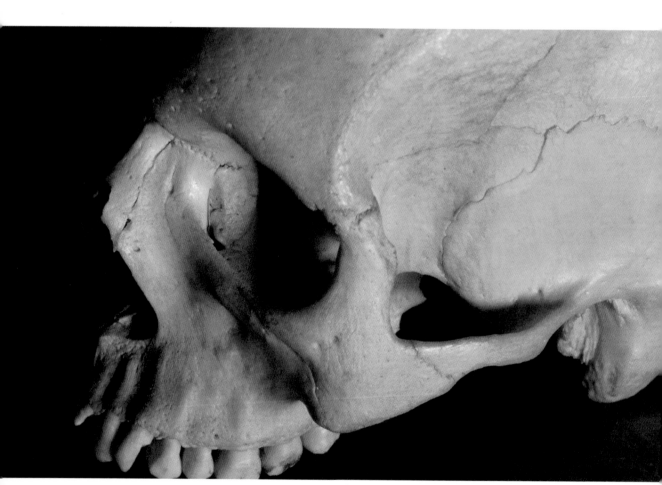

Bones may point to certain facts about a crime.

In the kidnapping case, two of the young woman's unique tattoos survived the inferno. So did her teeth. That pair of identifying marks, plus dental records, provided a name for the victim within hours of the blaze. Finding her body among the fire debris—especially in its specific location and in the condition it was in—first clued investigators to the intentional quality of this fire. Soon after, they found out why it happened—the motive.

Fire Starters: Common Motives

5

The woman we discussed in chapter 4 had been kidnapped for ransom by four male acquaintances and a close female friend. The group left her gagged and tied to a chair in the twenty-five-degree basement (−4°C) of an unheated, abandoned house without food, water, or even a blanket. They left her there while they went off to negotiate a ransom and attend to other details of their crime. (Obviously the motive for kidnapping was greed: money.) Nearly four days later, the men returned to find her seemingly lifeless body literally frozen to her chair.

Their victim looked like she did when they'd left her. The duct-tape bindings holding her mouth, wrists, and ankles were mostly intact, and her handcuffed hands were still behind her around a steel pole. She didn't move, she was cold to touch, and she didn't react to pain. The four young men thought she was dead. In reality, the twenty-year-old was unconscious and suffering from *hy-*

pothermia and dehydration. A forensic autopsy later proved she was still alive at this point.

Frantic and scared, the four scrambled to decide what to do next. In his book *Buried Alive*, author Kieran Crowley paraphrases their thinking: "Burn the whole place. This way there will be no fingerprints. . . . Just burn the house with her in it. It gets rid of all the evidence. . . . We can't get caught."

There's the motive: destroying every scrap of evidence to evade arrest and prosecution. Fire didn't destroy all the evidence, of course; it usually

Arson is sometimes used to cover up evidence of another crime.

doesn't. Two years later, after over 700 days of exhaustive forensic work—and on what would have been her twenty-second birthday—the first of the young victim's killers' verdicts came in: guilty of first-degree kidnapping, felony murder, depraved indifference, and arson.

Motivating Motives

According to the Oxford Dictionary, motive is "that which induces a person to act in a certain way." Webster's Dictionary defines it this way: "something (as a need or desire) that causes a person to act." Simply put, motive is the underlying reason we do whatever we do. We study because we want to learn or to get good grades; we make a snack because we're hungry or desire a specific food; these arsonists set fire to save their necks. Motive answers the question, "Why?"

The reasons people intentionally destroy property are many and varied, but there's always some benefit in it for them. In their minds, those perks can be financial, material, legal, physical, intellectual, emotional, psychological, religious, political, or even sexual. It is the thought of the payoff that motivates these criminals to act.

In his book Forensics for Dummies, D. P. Lyle lists the most common reasons arsonists and bombers resort to deliberate destruction:

1. to cover their tracks
2. to get money (insurance fraud)
3. psychological illness or disorder
4. to get even (revenge)
5. to end a life—their own or another's
6. to make a political statement or cause fear

CAREER SPOTLIGHT:
Forensic Accountants

A forensic accountant conducts financial investigations related to motive or identifying suspects. Detectives nearly always call one in when they suspect arson for profit.

Destroying Evidence

Many arsonists use fires to cover tracks of other crimes. The kidnapping case just discussed illustrates this motive perfectly. In that situation, four arsonists tried to erase any evidence of their part in the victim's abduction. Murderers, too, often try to disguise cause of death by burning their victims' bodies after they've otherwise killed them. Other arsonists seek to cover less extreme crimes like theft and embezzlement.

Let's say a group of employees steals electronic products from their employer's warehouse. They might torch the warehouse to avoid suspicion; the employers would never know any items were missing if everything burned. Or perhaps someone has been stealing money from a charity for which he works by falsifying financial records to show less income and pocketing the balance. That same person might burn down the entire office building just to destroy financial records. Motive—the driving benefit—in both of these arson fires would be to cover theft. Self-preservation is a powerful force.

Fraud

Fraud is another popular arena for arson/bombing motives. In fact, most arsons fall into this category. Perhaps a couple owns a restaurant that isn't doing well. Fast cash would bail them out of financial trouble. The business's fire insurance policy is for $500,000 and covers accidental causes. By burning down the restaurant through faking a fire accident, the owners hope to cash in on that $500,000. The motive here is purely financial: insurance fraud. Greed is a powerful force.

Another form of fraud is faking someone's death. Sometimes people just want to disappear. Maybe they want to leave their family and start a new life. Maybe they want to cash in on a life insurance policy. Maybe they want to escape something they must face, like the previously highlighted case about the couple who faked the husband's death to avoid his going to prison. Whatever the primary motive, faking a death is another form of fraud.

Mental Illness or Defect

Some individuals, though not many, have a pathological love of fire. These folks start fires simply because they love fire. They find its power, vitality, and beauty thrilling, exciting, stimulating, or (in rare instances) sexually arousing. Something about fire satisfies a deep-seated psychological need. Misguided thinking drives their actions. Because the motive is purely psychological, this kind of arson frequently graduates to a serial offense (in other words, one that is repeated again and again).

Insurance Fraud: Who Ultimately Pays?

Insurance works because companies collect money from all their customers in the form of monthly, quarterly, or annual payments called premiums to pay the few of their customers who actually file claims. False claims increase the number of those "few." The more claims the insurance company has to pay out, the more money it needs, so the more it must charge its customers to cover that cost.

For example, a pizza parlor needs fire insurance to be in business, and the owners' insurance bill goes up because less honest insurance customers have been filing false claims and getting away with it. The pizza place, in turn, has to charge its customers more for food in order to cover its increasing expenses. Ultimately, the consumer pays for insurance fraud.

Revenge

The desire to get even with a person, a group of people, a company, an organization, or even an entire ethnic group can be fierce enough to drive some arsonists and fire-bombers to torch homes, cars, neighborhoods, and properties. Their motive is anchored in hate, resentment, or a deeply rooted grudge. These burners want to inflict harm to settle a score. The payoff is usually purely emotional: satisfaction. Revenge tends to drive many fire-bombings.

Suicide or Murder

Usually when investigators find a homicide victim among fire debris, that person was dead before the blaze. Arsonists rarely use fire to kill themselves or others. Fire is simply too unpredictable for murder and too painful for suicide. Bombers are another story; they often desire to kill with their bombs. But usually a personal "cause" motivates them, not the sheer thrill of taking a life.

Championing a Cause

Sometimes a strongly held belief can drive someone to arson, like the religious zealot who firebombs an abortion clinic or the terrorist who bombs a plane or building. Bombs—not fire alone—are usually the weapon of choice with this motive. The driving force is the belief that his actions have a greater good. This arsonist serves a cause, not a personal agenda.

Those are the main six motives, with one glaring oversight—simple acts of vandalism.

Identifying the Perp

A host of statistics indicates that most fire-setters and bombers are male. Only about 6 percent are female, according to criminal profiler Dian Williams, president and CEO of the Center for Arson Research in Philadelphia, Pennsylvania. Furthermore, we know that arson fires in America are mostly motivated by potential profit. Even with such specific knowledge, discovering who the culprits are and bringing them to justice presents extraordinary problems in crimes of arson or bombing. The challenges here may be greater than in any other type of crime. One senior forensic scientist with Forensic Science Services, a company based in Oakville, Ontario, Canada, agrees: "Out of all crime probably arson is one of the easiest to commit. However, it's probably one of the most difficult to investigate and solve."

Identifying a suspect can be virtually impossible without understanding motive, especially if physical evidence is lacking. Thankfully, forensic criminalists, forensic psychiatrists, and psychological profilers can help. How? By understanding the human mind. When forensic "mind-hunters" study criminals as long and as intensively as they do, they come to realize that even though each crime is unique, human behavior is not. It fits into common, recognizable patterns.

Sometimes motive is obvious, as in arson-for-profit and arson-to-conceal crimes and firebombing-for-revenge. Conversely, motive becomes muddy and elusive in random acts of arson and bombing, those that are products of thrill fire-setters or serial bombers. How can patterns of behavior narrow that suspect field? Simply put, behavior reflects personality.

We all behave in certain ways every day, without being aware of it. At some point we don't even think about some behaviors because they've become engrained in us. They're simply part of who we are. Is your hair always in place? Are your dresser drawers tidy or chaotic? How about your locker? A person can tell a lot about another person by looking inside her purse, car, or closets.

Family history and individual personality shape the initial times we act in a specific way, then reinforce the behavior as time goes on. Criminal profilers train for years to understand the various histories and personalities behind criminal behavior.

Motivating the Criminal Mind

The U.S. National Center for the Analysis of Violent Crime classifies arson and bombing motives into six broad categories:

1. profit
2. vandalism
3. excitement
4. revenge
5. crime concealment
6. extremism

Of course any of the six can be subdivided. For instance, extremism may include acts of religious or political fanatics. Crime concealment may break down into arson covering murder or theft. Excitement can be as diverse as the one-time teen vandal who starts a fire for kicks and the serial fire-starter driven by sexual arousal.

When his brother identified Ted Kaczynski as the Unabomber, FBI profilers saw how perceptive they had been: white, loner, living reclusively, brilliant, and so on. Based on bomb-scene evidence, they had created a remarkably accurate portrait of a likely suspect. They just didn't have a name to attach to the profile. David Kaczynski gave them one.

Fanning the Flame

The world of arson and explosion investigations is a diverse one. Not only are there many individual forensic fields, but to complicate matters, each locality has its own way of doing things, including various job titles

Understanding an arsonist's motive helps in identifying the perpetrator.

CAREER SPOTLIGHT:
Forensic Criminalists Profilers/
Criminal Profilers/
Forensic Psychiatrists

Forensic Criminalists: These professionals analyze crime scenes from a psychological angle to determine potential motives and behavior during the crime.

Profilers/Criminal Profilers: These detectives create likely profiles of unknown suspects (age, race, gender, lifestyle, employment, family history, etc.) based on comparative evidence from serial crimes; they can sometimes predict what a serial offender will do based on the profile and established patterns.

Forensic Psychiatrists: Such doctors are usually brought in after investigators have identified a suspect. They assess witnesses, determine suspects' sanity and competence to stand trial, conduct psychological autopsies on suicide victims, and may also be involved in behavioral profiling. This career requires a medical degree in psychiatry.

Planning for the Future

If any of the career possibilities highlighted in this book interest you, find out more about them. Other books in this series explore select fields in much greater depth. Check online resources, related technical institutes, and local colleges. Visit law enforcement agencies; many host open houses. Doing your homework can clarify what is required for any given field and where you can obtain those requirements.

Some forensics jobs only require a strong interest in the field. Others require a medical degree. Many require board certification, while others have no certification requirements. One prerequisite, though, is true of every position: you can't have a criminal record. By definition, forensics—in any area, not just fire and explosion investigations—deals with matters of law, and to work in law enforcement you can't have a rap sheet.

and responsibilities that depend on budgets, personnel, and facilities. Regardless, no one forensic field investigates and solves fire or explosion cases alone. From conducting autopsies to viewing singed documents, from profiling criminals to taking accelerant samples at the scene, arson investigation involves many fascinating disciplines.

Remember: wherever we go, we leave a little bit of ourselves behind and, in turn, pick up bits of other people, places, and things. The same is true of the arsonist or bomber. Finding out who, what, when, where, how, and why as it relates to the crime is what fire investigation is all about.

Glossary

accelerants: Substances used to intensify a fire.

clandestine: Secret, and often illegal.

compounds: Things made by combining two or more different chemical elements.

control sample: A sample participating in an experiment, but not involved in the procedures affecting the rest of the experiment.

hypothermia: Abnormally low body temperature.

insidious: Stealthy, treacherous, harmful, destructive.

joists: Parallel beams that support a ceiling, floor, or roof.

malicious: Deliberately harmful.

Molotov cocktail: A crude bomb, usually made of a bottle filled with a flammable liquid and a wick that is lit just before the bottle is thrown.

suppression: The act of pressing down or stopping natural growth.

transient: Temporary.

Further Reading

Axelrod, Alan, and Guy Antinozzi. *The Complete Idiot's Guide to Criminal Investigation*. Indianapolis, Ind.: Alpha Books, 2003.

Camenson, Blythe. *Opportunities in Forensic Science Careers*. Lincolnwood, Ill.: VGM Career Books, 2001.

Campbell, Andrea. *Forensic Science: Evidence, Clues, and Investigation*. Philadelphia, Pa.: Chelsea House Publishers, 2000.

Evans, Colin. *The Casebook of Forensic Detection: How Science Solved 100 of the World's Most Baffling Crimes*. New York: Berkley Trade, 2007.

Faith, Nicholas. *Blaze: The Forensics of Fire*. New York: St. Martin's Press, 1999.

Gorrell, Gena K. *Catching Fire: The Story of Firefighting*. Toronto, Ontario/Plattsburgh, N.Y.: Tundra Books, 1999.

Genge, Ngaire E. *The Forensic Casebook: The Science of Crime Scene Investigation*. New York and Toronto: Ballantine Publishing Group and Random House of Canada Limited, 2002.

Houde, John. *Crime Lab: A Guide for Nonscientists*. Ventura, Calif.: Calico Press, 1999.

Lyle, Douglas P. *Forensics for Dummies*. Hoboken, N.J.: Wiley Publishing, 2004.

Masoff, Joy. *Fire!* New York: Scholastic, 2002.

Owen, David. *Hidden Evidence: Forty True Crimes and How Forensic Science Helped Solve Them*. Willowdale, Ontario/Buffalo, N.Y.: Firefly Books Ltd., 2000.

Zonderman, Jon. *Beyond the Crime Lab: The New Science of Investigation*. New York: John Wiley & Sons, Inc., 1999.

For More Information

Arson Dogs
www.workingdogs.com/doc0130.htm

Canadian Association of Arson Investigators (CAFI)
www.cafi.ca

Court TV's Crime Library
www.crimelibrary.com

Federal Bureau of Investigation (FBI)
www.fbi.gov

National Fire Protection Association
www.nfpa.org

InterFIRE
www.interfire.org

National Center for Forensic Science (NCFS)
www.ncfs.org

U.S. Department of Justice:
Bureau of Alcohol, Tobacco, Firearms, and Explosives (ATF)
www.atf.gov

U.S. Fire Administration
www.usfa.fema.gov

Publisher's note:
The websites listed on these pages were active at the time of publication. The publisher is not responsible for websites that have changed their addresses or discontinued operation since the date of publication. The publisher will review and update the website list upon each reprint.

Index

Picture Credits

Corbis: p. 82

Corel: pp. 24, 54, 86, 89

MK Bassett-Harvey: p. 76

Photos.com: pp. 12, 17, 20, 23, 32, 34, 39, 41, 44, 57, 67, 69, 74, 77, 81, 84, 90, 94, 102

To the best knowledge of the publisher, all other images are in the public domain. If any image has been inadvertently uncredited, please notify Vestal Creative Services, Vestal, New York 13850, so that rectification can be made for future printings.

Biographies

AUTHOR

Jean Ford is a freelance author, writer, award-winning illustrator, and public speaker. Internationally recognized, her work includes writing for periodicals from the United States to China, and speaking to audiences from as close as her tri-state area to as far away as Africa. Although she generally writes and speaks on nonfiction topics, Jean also enjoys writing and illustrating children's books.

SERIES CONSULTANTS

Carla Miller Noziglia is Senior Forensic Advisor for the U.S. Department of Justice, International Criminal Investigative Training Assistant Program. A Fellow of the American Academy of Forensic Sciences, Ms. Noziglia served as chair of the board of Trustees of the Forensic Science Foundation. Her work has earned her many honors and commendations, including Distinguished Fellow from the American Academy of Forensic Sciences (2003) and the Paul L. Kirk Award from the American Academy of Forensic Sciences Criminalistics Section. Ms. Noziglia's publications include *The Real Crime Lab* (coeditor, 2005), *So You Want to be a Forensic Scientist* (coeditor, 2003), and contributions to *Drug Facilitated Sexual Assault* (2001), *Convicted by Juries, Exonerated by Science: Case Studies in the Use of DNA* (1996), and the *Journal of Police Science* (1989). She is on the editorial board of the *Journal for Forensic Identification*.

Jay Siegel is Director of the Forensic and Investigative Sciences Program at Indiana University-Purdue University, Indianapolis and Chair of the Department of Chemistry and Chemical Biology. He holds a Ph.D. in Analytical Chemistry from George Washington University. He worked for three years at the Virginia Bureau of Forensic Sciences, analyzing drugs, fire residues, and trace evidence. From 1980 to 2004 he was professor of forensic chemistry and director of the forensic science program at Michigan State University in the School of Criminal Justice. Dr. Siegel has testified over 200 times as an expert witness in twelve states, Federal Court and Military Court. He is editor in chief of the *Encyclopedia of Forensic Sciences*, author of *Forensic Science: A Beginner's Guide and Fundamentals of Forensic Science*, and he has more than thirty publications in forensic science journals. Dr. Siegel was awarded the 2005 Paul Kirk Award for lifetime achievement in forensic science. In February 2009, he was named Distinguished Fellow by the American Academy of Forensic Sciences.